The Notebook for the Christian Woman

# In Her Own Words

## The Notebook for the Christian Woman

The Notebook for the Christian Woman

# In Her Own Words

## The Notebook for the Christian Woman

**By
Minister Onedia N. Gage**

The Notebook for the Christian Woman

## Other Books by Onedia N. Gage, M. Ed., MBA

Are You Ready for 9<sup>th</sup> Grade . . . Again? A Family's Guide to Success

As We Grow Together Daily Devotional for Expectant Couples

As We Grow Together Prayer Journal for Expectant Couples

The Blue Print: Poetry for the Soul

From Two to One: The Notebook for Couples

In Purple Ink: Poetry for the Spirit

Living a Whole Life: Sermons which Prompt, Provoke and Promote Life

Love Letters to God from a Teenage Girl

The Measure of a Woman: The Details of Her Soul

The Notebook: For Me, About Me, By Me

The Notebook for the Christian Teen

On This Journey Daily Devotional for Young People

On This Journey Prayer Journal for Young People

One Day More Than We Deserve Daily Devotional for the Growing Christian

One Day More Than We Deserve Prayer Journal for the Growing Christian

Promises, Promises: A Christian Novel

Tools for These Times: Timely Sermons for Uncertain Times

With An Anointed Voice: The Power of Prayer

Yielded and Submitted: A Woman's Journey for a Life Dedicated to God

Yielded and Submitted: A Woman's Journey for a Life Dedicated to God An Intimate Study

Yielded and Submitted: A Woman's Journey for a Life Dedicated to God Prayers and Journal

The Notebook for the Christian Woman

## Library of Congress

In Her Own Words:

The Notebook For the Christian Woman

All Rights Reserved © 2014

Onedia N. Gage

No part of this of book may be reproduced or transmitted in
Any form or by any means, graphic, electronic, or mechanical,
Including photocopying, recording, taping, or by any
Information storage or retrieval system, without the
Permission in writing from the publisher.

Purple Ink, Inc. Press

For Information address:
Purple Ink, Inc
P O Box 41232
Houston, TX 77241
www.purpleink.net
www.onediagage.com

ISBN:

979-1-939119-38-4

Printed in United States

# Dedication

Hillary
for the woman you will become

Nehemiah
for the woman you will marry

Every woman I will meet!
Every woman I will minister to!
Every woman I will pray for!

Every woman who is in need of healing!
Every woman who is in need of prayer!
Every woman who is in need of rescue!
Every woman who is in need of recovery!
Every woman who is in need of restoration!
Every woman who is in need of dreams!

Every woman who is in need of LOVE!

The Notebook for the Christian Woman

In Her Own Words

# God's Words

Proverbs 31:10-31 (NIV)

**Epilogue: The Wife of Noble Character**

<sup>10</sup> [a]A wife of noble character who can find?
  She is worth far more than rubies.
<sup>11</sup> Her husband has full confidence in her
  and lacks nothing of value.
<sup>12</sup> She brings him good, not harm,
  all the days of her life.
<sup>13</sup> She selects wool and flax
  and works with eager hands.
<sup>14</sup> She is like the merchant ships,
  bringing her food from afar.
<sup>15</sup> She gets up while it is still night;
  she provides food for her family
  and portions for her female servants.
<sup>16</sup> She considers a field and buys it;
  out of her earnings she plants a vineyard.
<sup>17</sup> She sets about her work vigorously;
  her arms are strong for her tasks.
<sup>18</sup> She sees that her trading is profitable,
  and her lamp does not go out at night.
<sup>19</sup> In her hand she holds the distaff
  and grasps the spindle with her fingers.
<sup>20</sup> She opens her arms to the poor
  and extends her hands to the needy.
<sup>21</sup> When it snows, she has no fear for her household;
  for all of them are clothed in scarlet.
<sup>22</sup> She makes coverings for her bed;
  she is clothed in fine linen and purple.
<sup>23</sup> Her husband is respected at the city gate,
  where he takes his seat among the elders of the land.
<sup>24</sup> She makes linen garments and sells them,
  and supplies the merchants with sashes.

# The Notebook for the Christian Woman

²⁵ She is clothed with strength and dignity;
   she can laugh at the days to come.
²⁶ She speaks with wisdom,
   and faithful instruction is on her tongue.
²⁷ She watches over the affairs of her household
   and does not eat the bread of idleness.
²⁸ Her children arise and call her blessed;
   her husband also, and he praises her:
²⁹ "Many women do noble things,
   but you surpass them all."
³⁰ Charm is deceptive, and beauty is fleeting;
   but a woman who fears the LORD is to be praised.
³¹ Honor her for all that her hands have done,
   and let her works bring her praise at the city gate.

## Luke 12:43-48 (NIV)

⁴³ And a woman was there who had been subject to bleeding for twelve years,[c] but no one could heal her. ⁴⁴ She came up behind him and touched the edge of his cloak, and immediately her bleeding stopped.

⁴⁵ "Who touched me?" Jesus asked.

When they all denied it, Peter said, "Master, the people are crowding and pressing against you."

⁴⁶ But Jesus said, "Someone touched me; I know that power has gone out from me."

⁴⁷ Then the woman, seeing that she could not go unnoticed, came trembling and fell at his feet. In the presence of all the people, she told why she had touched him and how she had been instantly healed. ⁴⁸ Then he said to her, "Daughter, your faith has healed you. Go in peace."

## Luke 7:36-39, 46-50 (NIV)

**Jesus Anointed by a Sinful Woman**

[36] When one of the Pharisees invited Jesus to have dinner with him, he went to the Pharisee's house and reclined at the table. [37] A woman in that town who lived a sinful life learned that Jesus was eating at the Pharisee's house, so she came there with an alabaster jar of perfume. [38] As she stood behind him at his feet weeping, she began to wet his feet with her tears. Then she wiped them with her hair, kissed them and poured perfume on them.

[39] When the Pharisee who had invited him saw this, he said to himself, "If this man were a prophet, he would know who is touching him and what kind of woman she is—that she is a sinner."

[46] You did not put oil on my head, but she has poured perfume on my feet. [47] Therefore, I tell you, her many sins have been forgiven—as her great love has shown. But whoever has been forgiven little loves little."

[48] Then Jesus said to her, "Your sins are forgiven."

[49] The other guests began to say among themselves, "Who is this who even forgives sins?"

[50] Jesus said to the woman, "Your faith has saved you; go in peace."

The Notebook for the Christian Woman

14 | Minister Gage

# In Her Own Words

Dear God,

Lord God, I pray for us as women daily. I am a woman and I need You! As women, we need to hear from You. Lord, I thank You for making us women. We have so much to do in this world but there are times when we let those things take over us. Lord, Your word says that You would fight my battles if I would just be still. I think that I need to understand what Your fight looks like so that I may be still enough to see the fight You are already fighting for me.

Lord, thank You for forgiving me for my sins and there are so many of them. I really love You but You may not know it because I am disobedient so often. I thank You for being God and God alone.
Lord, please teach me how to worship You better where my worship is pleasing to Your sight. I thank You right now Lord for loving me better than I could ever love myself.

Lord, thank You for holding me when I am sad, lonely and broken. Thank You for keeping me while I am in the valley and reminding me of Your presence and omnipotence when I am on the mountain. I am going to need Your hand of protection around me as I progress because I am certain to get myself in some trouble as I travel on this journey.

Lord, as I forgive others, help me to forgive myself. I need to forgive myself so that I can love and forgive others. Lord, teach me to love better and more completely and more authentically. Lord, I really want to be the best woman that You have made me. I need You, God!

Lord, thank You for time to study, the craving for me to seek Your face and Your heart and the ability to pray to You. Lord, help me to pray to You with all of my heart. Thank You for allowing me to come to You with all that I am and all that I am not. I need Your help with opening my heart to Your Words, Your message, Your messenger and all that You have in store for me.

I pray for these blessings in Jesus' name.
Amen.

The Notebook for the Christian Woman

## In Her Own Words

Dear Woman:

The Notebook is for you, about you and by you, where God, Jesus and the Holy Spirit will walk you through your life. I never feel the ability to be completely transparent because that is not politically or culturally correct, however with God there is freedom to be YOU! You can be You because God created you and He can correct those areas where you are weak or offensive or outrageous. God will do that lovingly and with the promise that life will be better when He is done pruning you.

I know that I often reach for God and wonder if He is there, listening and willing to save my sorry self from my own entanglements. And God is there. I know that we have a long way to go on this journey. I just know that God punishes the sin and preserves the sinner. The walk we have as a woman is unique and completely phenomenal and with plenty of pressure. God is here and has never left us alone.

Search for yourself: your original, genuine self. God deserves your best self. Various things have altered this within, however, you could return to the factory settings which God designed. Don't neglect this opportunity to grow and return to you: your awesome, joyful, authentic, and fabulous self.

Gage's definition of the Measure of a Woman: The fullness of that woman from head to heart to toes. This definition includes her work, her family and her love. This Measure includes the depth, breadth, height, and width of her love capacity and all other characteristics. This encompasses the resilience of a woman. This measure also explains why she is defined as a woman. Her profound acts and wisdom and the love she experiences which introduces the hurts she encounters but eventually endures. Use your words to understand your fullest measure!

# The Notebook for the Christian Woman

Use this Notebook to express your feelings, fears, and what you think about yourself and God. The questions are provocative, pensive, piercing, productive, and powerful. Do not cut yourself short. Leave it all on the paper. Use your words. Give yourself permission to grow through this experience. Look at your life and consider the options. Decide to live and escape that which holds you hostage, including yourself.

I look forward to hearing from you. Feel free to share with me as you journey. You can follow me on twitter @onediangage, email onediagage@onediagage.com, facebook.com/onediagageministries, blogtalkradio.com/onediagage, and youtube.com/onediagage.

I can hardly wait!

In His Service!

*Onedia N. Gage*

Onedia N. Gage
www.onediagage.com

In Her Own Words

## Instructions for Use

### Write.

**In Her Own Words: The Notebook for the Christian Woman** was developed to provide you with an avenue of expression. It was adapted from the original version, The Notebook. As a classroom teacher, I had a student who was experiencing some difficulties with his life. **The Notebook** was created just for him. Upon reflection, I decided that the Christian Woman needed one as well. You should respond to the questions honestly. Feel free to be transparent.

### Share.

Share or don't share. Completely your choice. I find that when we write our feelings down, they are easier to share.

### Save.

Save your own life. We need to get to a point of understanding ourselves so that we can function in a controlled environment. We want to respond when we have thought carefully and considered wisely the consequences of our actions. If we answer these questions honestly for ourselves, then we can be address our issues in a transparent, which will give us an understanding of what we need to grow and mature into as a woman. Stop sabotaging yourself and your success.

### Time.

The time you spend in this notebook is for you. Use it selfishly and wisely!

In Her Own Words
The Notebook for the Christian Woman

The Notebook for the Christian Woman

*In Her Own Words*

# THE WOMAN IN THE PHOTO
## By Onedia N. Gage

She's pretty
    . . . but what's behind her eyes
She's glamorous
    . . . but what's on her mind
She has diva attitude and everything
    . . . but what makes her happy, angry and sad
She's smiling
    . . . but is she really
She's almost laughing
    . . . but is it authentic
She appears happy
    . . . but what does she need

The woman in the photo
Investigate her
Probe her for the details
Pay attention to the subtleties
Precise are her moves
Poised are her moods

Is that vision of beauty
    Hiding hurt
    Harboring anger
    Healing from harm
Take note of the woman in the photo
Each detail of her being
Test for her authenticity

## The Notebook for the Christian Woman

The woman in the photo
Requires your attention
Requests your affection
Resigns for love
Recognizes your fear
Relinquishes her power
Retaliates from hate
Responds with care
Relies on honesty
Relishes in peace

The woman in the photo
    Is real
    Is a reality
    Is a dream realized

The Woman in the Photo.


Reprinted from <u>The Measure of a Woman: The Details of Her Soul</u>

## Table of Contents

| | |
|---|---|
| Letters | 9 |
| Poem: "The Woman in the Photo" | 23 |
| The Questions | 25 |
| Appendix | 181 |
|     Your Testimony | 183 |
|     The Names of God | 185 |
|     Prayer Directions | 187 |
|     Prayer Request List/Journal | 188 |
|     Favorite Scriptures | 193 |
|     Goals | 200 |
|     Mission | 202 |
|     Vision | 205 |
|     Values | 209 |
|     Dreams | 211 |
| Resources | 215 |
| Acknowledgements | 217 |

The Notebook for the Christian Woman

In Her Own Words

# The Questions

The Notebook for the Christian Woman

## In Her Own Words

What is your definition of a woman?
Are you that definition?
How did you reach that definition?
Who helped you develop your definition of you as a woman?
Is God pleased with that definition?

___
___
___
___
___
___
___
___
___
___
___
___
___
___

# The Notebook for the Christian Woman

Who are you?
Who does God say you are? How does God define you?
How did you reach that definition?

## In Her Own Words

How is this definition different from what God made you to be?

Is your definition of who you are defined by others? Who? Why?

How much do you rely on God for your definition of yourself?

### The Notebook for the Christian Woman

Does God approve of your definition?

Is your definition of yourself aligned with God's?

What can you do to abandon that definition if it does not align with God's definition?

Why or why not?

_____
_____
_____
_____
_____
_____
_____
_____
_____
_____
_____
_____
_____
_____

## In Her Own Words

Are you comfortable with who you are? Why or why not?

The Notebook for the Christian Woman

How are you defined by others? How do you know?
How did they reach that definition?
Are you comfortable with that definition? Why or why not?
Are you doing anything to change that definition?

_____
_____
_____
_____
_____
_____
_____
_____
_____
_____
_____
_____
_____
_____
_____

## In Her Own Words

What would you change about yourself?
Why is that an important change?
Who supports that change?

# The Notebook for the Christian Woman

What will be the outcome of that change?
Will God be pleased with that change(s)?
Who are these changes really for: you, them or God?

In Her Own Words

What makes you happy?
What happens when you are happy?
Who do you let affect your happiness? Why?

# The Notebook for the Christian Woman

Are you joyful?

Do you understand joy?

What is the difference between joy and happiness?

What is the source of your joy?

Who do you know that has joy or is joyful?

_____
_____
_____
_____
_____
_____
_____
_____
_____
_____
_____
_____
_____

## In Her Own Words

What disappoints God?
What do you do to disappoint God?
What disappoints you?
What happens when God is disappointed?
What happens when you are disappointed?

_____
_____
_____
_____
_____
_____
_____
_____
_____
_____
_____
_____
_____

# The Notebook for the Christian Woman

Who is God to you?

What do you know about God (names, attributes, ways, etc.)?

_____
_____
_____
_____
_____
_____
_____
_____
_____
_____
_____
_____
_____
_____
_____
_____
_____
_____
_____

## In Her Own Words

Who is Jesus Christ to you?

What do you know about Jesus Christ (names, characteristics, behavior, etc.)?

_____
_____
_____
_____
_____
_____
_____
_____
_____
_____
_____
_____
_____
_____
_____
_____

# The Notebook for the Christian Woman

Who is the Holy Spirit to you?

What do you know about the Holy Spirit (definition, role, characteristics, etc.)?

_____
_____
_____
_____
_____
_____
_____
_____
_____
_____
_____
_____
_____
_____
_____

## In Her Own Words

Is your Christian education important to you? Why or why not?

Do you take classes at church?

Do you attend women's conferences at your church or others?

How do you apply what you learn?

_____
_____
_____
_____
_____
_____
_____
_____
_____
_____
_____
_____
_____
_____
_____
_____

# The Notebook for the Christian Woman

How does God define success?

How do you define success?

What can happen to align those definitions so that they are closer?

_____
_____
_____
_____
_____
_____
_____
_____
_____
_____
_____
_____
_____
_____
_____

## In Her Own Words

How do you know that Christ loves you?
How much does Christ love you?
How much do you love Christ?
Why do you doubt God's love for you?

# THE HANDKERCHIEF
## By Onedia N. Gage

Tears of turmoil
Tears of triumph
How many tears have you
Washed from that handkerchief

The handkerchief would say
If it spoke
I dry each tear
Each tear that falls to her blouse
Each tear that crosses the bridge
To the eyelashes
But I told her that these
Tears are not for her

I remind her that each
Tear demands a testimony
Someone watching needs to see those tears
They need to see the shedding
Of the bondage of the storm

Tears evident of storm-stirring
Testimony is evidence of storm-shedding
The handkerchief shared that the
Tears are all different
She carries emotions inside which
She never shares

I stay by her side all night while
She dabs her face to catch the falling tears

One day she gave me away
To someone who had her same hurt
Then I became her testimony

She shared my comforting ability

## In Her Own Words

She cries
God heals
I comfort

She shares her testimony
She tells of how I've blessed
Those tears are gone
New ones come
But she grows by passing me on.


Reprinted from <u>The Blue Print: Poetry for the Soul</u>

The Notebook for the Christian Woman

When did you first meet Jesus?
How did meeting Jesus change your life?

_____
_____
_____
_____
_____
_____
_____
_____
_____
_____
_____
_____
_____
_____
_____
_____

**In Her Own Words**

Do you pray?
Do you know how to pray?
How did you learn to pray?

# The Notebook for the Christian Woman

Why do you pray?
Who do you pray for? Make a list.
Who knows that you pray? How do they know?
Do others ask you to pray for them?

In Her Own Words

Who do you know that prays?
Do you listen to them pray?
Do you ask that prayer warrior to pray for you?
Do you ask that prayer warrior to pray with you?

# The Notebook for the Christian Woman

What are you praying for?
What are you asking God for?
Do you pray during the storms in your life?

_____
_____
_____
_____
_____
_____
_____
_____
_____
_____
_____
_____
_____
_____

## In Her Own Words

When have you seen God answer your prayers?
What prayer(s) did God answer?
What did God say?

Define friendship.
What are the characteristics of a friend?
Are you a great friend?
What can you do to be a better friend?
Do you know that Jesus is your friend?

In Her Own Words

Do your friends know that you are a Christian?
How do they know you are a Christian?

# The Notebook for the Christian Woman

When Christ said He was your friend, how did that make you feel?

Do you understand why Jesus said that He is our friend(s)?

_____
_____
_____
_____
_____
_____
_____
_____
_____
_____
_____
_____
_____
_____
_____

In Her Own Words

Who have you invited to visit church?

How often do you invite someone to visit church?

# The Notebook for the Christian Woman

*What do you want God to call you to do?*

*What are your spiritual gifts?*

_____

_____

_____

_____

_____

_____

_____

_____

_____

_____

_____

_____

_____

_____

_____

In Her Own Words

What are you trying to avoid that God has called you to do?

# The Notebook for the Christian Woman

Is there anything that would cause you to walk away from God?

**In Her Own Words**

How do you explain why God is real to you?
Do you feel comfortable explaining this about God?

_____
_____
_____
_____
_____
_____
_____
_____
_____
_____
_____
_____
_____
_____
_____
_____

# The Notebook for the Christian Woman

What do you worry about?

What does God say about worry?

## In Her Own Words

What burdens you?

What does Jesus say about your burdens?

Why is it so difficult to give Jesus your burdens?

Why are you holding on to them?

_____

_____

_____

_____

_____

_____

_____

_____

_____

_____

_____

_____

_____

_____

# The Notebook for the Christian Woman

Does God respond when we are moody and temperamental?

What determines your mood each day?

## In Her Own Words

Who/What makes you angry?

What determines how long you stay angry?

What do you do to resolve that anger?

What does God want us to do when we are angry?

What did Jesus do when He was angry?

Why are you still angry?

_____

_____

_____

_____

_____

_____

_____

_____

_____

_____

_____

_____

# The Notebook for the Christian Woman

As the matriarch, do you fully understand your role?

Do you fully operate in your role?

Do you seek assistance in your role when trouble or victory is present?

_____
_____
_____
_____
_____
_____
_____
_____
_____
_____
_____
_____
_____
_____
_____

## In Her Own Words

How do you shape your family culture?
How does your family respond?
How did you decide what your goals are for your family?

# The Notebook for the Christian Woman

Do you know the story of Cain and Abel?

How do you feel about your family?

Why?

Is there a particular event that caused these feelings?

Do you have a similar situation in your family history?

How can you stop this from happening as the matriarch of the family?

_____
_____
_____
_____
_____
_____
_____
_____
_____
_____
_____
_____

## In Her Own Words

Do you know the story of Joseph and his brothers?
How does your family feel about you? Why?
Is there a particular event that caused these feelings?
What would you do in this situation if you were Joseph?

_____
_____
_____
_____
_____
_____
_____
_____
_____
_____
_____
_____
_____
_____

# The Notebook for the Christian Woman

Do you know the story of Abraham, Sarah, Haggar, Issac and Ishmael?
How is your family defined? Feel free to draw a picture, if desired.
Which woman do you identity most with?
In the same spirit of desperation, would you follow the example of Sarah?
How would you have handled that?

_____
_____
_____
_____
_____
_____
_____
_____
_____
_____
_____
_____
_____
_____

In Her Own Words

Do you know the story of Noah?
How do you feel about your family structure/dynamics?
What if you had been Noah's wife during the flood?

_____
_____
_____
_____
_____
_____
_____
_____
_____
_____
_____
_____
_____
_____
_____

# The Notebook for the Christian Woman

Do you know the story of Joseph, Mary, and Jesus?
If you could pick your family, would you pick the one you have? Why?
If not, who would you pick as a family? Why?

_____
_____
_____
_____
_____
_____
_____
_____
_____
_____
_____
_____
_____
_____
_____

# In Her Own Words

Could you have been picked as Mary?

Could you be the mother of Jesus?

How do you cultivate and encourage greatness in your children right now?

_____
_____
_____
_____
_____
_____
_____
_____
_____
_____
_____
_____
_____
_____
_____
_____

### The Notebook for the Christian Woman

Do you know the story of David?
What are important family values for you?
How did you learn these values?
Are these currently functioning in your home?

## In Her Own Words

How do you feel about David and Bathsheba?

What would you do in Bathsheba's position?

How can we avoid those situations?

# The Notebook for the Christian Woman

Do you know the story of Job?
What should a family do and be?
What makes someone family?

**In Her Own Words**

Tell your Job story.
Job's wife: What should she be doing?
What would you do in her situation?

_____
_____
_____
_____
_____
_____
_____
_____
_____
_____
_____
_____
_____
_____

# The Notebook for the Christian Woman

Do you know the story of Ruth to David to Jesus?

What is your family legacy?

Consider family education, businesses owned, homeownership, and overall activities.

With Ruth as a guide, what would you to change your life or add to your current life?

_____
_____
_____
_____
_____
_____
_____
_____
_____
_____
_____
_____
_____

## In Her Own Words

Who is your favorite family member?

Why?

How much time do you spend with him/her?

What kind of activities do you do when you are together?

What do you teach them?

What do they teach you?

_____
_____
_____
_____
_____
_____
_____
_____
_____
_____
_____
_____
_____

# The Notebook for the Christian Woman

Consider the verses Titus 2:1-8.
Do you have a person that does this for you?
Who are you a Titus 2 woman to?

_____
_____
_____
_____
_____
_____
_____
_____
_____
_____
_____
_____
_____
_____
_____

In Her Own Words

# DIVA, HOW ARE YOU?
### By Onedia N. Gage

I looked into your eyes the other day and I didn't like what I saw.
I hadn't looked into your deep, intellectual eyes in awhile,
So when I did, I was surprised that I saw hurt and pain and loneliness.

So Diva, what's wrong? What are we going to do?
I can't afford for you to smile into a slump or a lull or a real depression.
I can't afford for you to take an emotional hiatus or even a break.

So Diva, what can I do to help you?
Do we need to come and clean your house?
Or watch your kids?
Or help you cook some food?
Do you need a night out with your significant other?
Do you need a night out with us?
What do you need?
What can we do?

I see the smile that you want to be real.
I know that you hoped I missed the emptiness I saw or the coldness behind the eyes.
But the truth is that I did see your fear and your disdain.
That was my call to help.
That was my cue to start a rescue mission.
That was my sign to start an intervention.
The intervention where we restore your faith in God,
Hope for the impossible, love for yourself, and
Trust in things and those who matter most.

# The Notebook for the Christian Woman

I looked into those eyes the other day.
The hurt stayed on my mind.

Forgive me if we have overstepped our perceived boundaries but we are your real friends.
I would rather have you here and be able to make up from your scowl than not have you here at all.

Diva, we love you! Please let us help you!

Reprinted from <u>The Measure of a Woman: The Details of Her Soul</u>

## In Her Own Words

Do you have a role model?
Do you admire their relationship with Christ?
Who is it?
How did you select that person as your role model?

# The Notebook for the Christian Woman

Are rich and poor important to you? How do you define rich and poor? Are you rich or poor?
How does God address riches?
Do you let rich/poor define who you are?
Are you willing to adopt God's definition of riches and abandon your own?

_____
_____
_____
_____
_____
_____
_____
_____
_____
_____
_____
_____
_____
_____

**In Her Own Words**

What does God say about money?

Do you need help managing your money?

Is it a consistent struggle?

_____

_____

_____

_____

_____

_____

_____

_____

_____

_____

_____

_____

_____

_____

# The Notebook for the Christian Woman

*Should you feel guilty about God blessing you with money if others close to you do not have enough? How do you help those in need?*

_____
_____
_____
_____
_____
_____
_____
_____
_____
_____
_____
_____
_____
_____

## In Her Own Words

What would do you with $500,000?

Would you give 10% to the church?

Who would you tell first?

Who do you know or know of with this amount of money?

_____
_____
_____
_____
_____
_____
_____
_____
_____
_____
_____
_____
_____
_____

# The Notebook for the Christian Woman

What would you do with $1 million?

Would you give 10% to the church?

Who would you tell first?

Who do you know or know of with this amount of money?

___

## In Her Own Words

What would you do with $10 million?

Would you give 10% to the church?

Who would you tell first?

Who do you know or know of with that amount of money?

_____
_____
_____
_____
_____
_____
_____
_____
_____
_____
_____
_____
_____
_____

The Notebook for the Christian Woman

Who does God want us to value?
Who do you value?
Why?

_____
_____
_____
_____
_____
_____
_____
_____
_____
_____
_____
_____
_____
_____
_____

### In Her Own Words

What does God want us to value?

What do you value?

Why?

# The Notebook for the Christian Woman

Who is your best friend? Why?
What does God say about friends?
How do you spend your time together?
How did you meet?
How long have you been friends?

_____
_____
_____
_____
_____
_____
_____
_____
_____
_____
_____
_____
_____
_____

**In Her Own Words**

Do your friend(s) know Christ?

If not, do you plan to share Jesus with your best friend?

# The Notebook for the Christian Woman

What has been the best thing that God has ever done to/for you?

Why?

_____
_____
_____
_____
_____
_____
_____
_____
_____
_____
_____
_____
_____
_____

In Her Own Words

What has been the second best thing that God has ever done to/for you?

Why?

The Notebook for the Christian Woman

>What age do you first remember listening to God?
>What age do you first remember knowing God and Jesus?
>What did you first learn about Christ?
>What does God say to you now?

_____
_____
_____
_____
_____
_____
_____
_____
_____
_____
_____
_____
_____
_____

In Her Own Words

What is the worst aspect of your childhood? Why?
Did you share this with God?
What did God say?

# The Notebook for the Christian Woman

What is your favorite part of your knowledge of God?

Why?

## In Her Own Words

What is the worst thing you have ever experienced?
Did you tell Jesus about it? What did Jesus say?
Who did you share that with? What did they say?

# The Notebook for the Christian Woman

How do you share that Jesus died for your sins?

Have you ever experienced the death of someone close to you in age?

Have you ever experienced the death of someone in your family that you thought you could not live without?

Who? How did it make you feel?

_____
_____
_____
_____
_____
_____
_____
_____
_____
_____
_____
_____
_____
_____

# In Her Own Words

How long did it take you to recover from the death of that person(s)?
Did you blame or hate God for that death? Why?
How long did it take for you to stop being angry?

# The Notebook for the Christian Woman

Is suicide a sin?

Is it forgivable by God?

Are your issues so much bigger than God that you consider such a permanent option?

What can you do to prevent your child from considering suicide?

_____
_____
_____
_____
_____
_____
_____
_____
_____
_____
_____
_____
_____

## In Her Own Words

Has your heart ever been broken? By who?
Did you ask Jesus to heal you from that hurt?
Has the hurt subsided? Are you healed?
How long did it take to heal?
Do you hold others accountable for that hurt?

_____
_____
_____
_____
_____
_____
_____
_____
_____
_____
_____
_____
_____

The Notebook for the Christian Woman

What does Paul say about love?
Have you ever been 'in love'?
How did you feel when you were 'in love'?
How long did it last?
Do you look forward to it happening again?

_____
_____
_____
_____
_____
_____
_____
_____
_____
_____
_____
_____
_____

**In Her Own Words**

How does God define love?

How do you define love?

# The Notebook for the Christian Woman

Who loves you?
Whom do you love?
Is love important to you?
Why?

In Her Own Words

How does Jesus know that you love Him?
Obedience? Words? Actions? Service to others?
What can you do to let Jesus know better that you love Him?

_____
_____
_____
_____
_____
_____
_____
_____
_____
_____
_____
_____
_____
_____
_____

# The Notebook for the Christian Woman

What is important to God for you?

What is important to you (either material or intangible)?

How far apart is that definition from God's?

What can't you live without?

Why?

_____
_____
_____
_____
_____
_____
_____
_____
_____
_____
_____
_____
_____

## In Her Own Words

Why did God make you a parent?

What does God say we are to do as parents?

Are you a good parent?

The Notebook for the Christian Woman

Could you be a better parent?
When and why is parenting them hard for you?

In Her Own Words

Do you ever question God's will for and plan for you?

# The Notebook for the Christian Woman

Who is your favorite person at church?

Who do you admire at church?

Why?

In Her Own Words

What is your favorite scripture(s)?

# The Notebook for the Christian Woman

## What is your favorite part of church?
## Why?

**In Her Own Words**

Who is your favorite Biblical character?
Why?

# The Notebook for the Christian Woman

Who is your favorite Christian actor/actress/TV personality/musician?

Why?

If you met them, what would you say?

How would you want to spend that time?

**In Her Own Words**

What will you say to God when you get to heaven?

The Notebook for the Christian Woman

What questions do you have of God?

_____
_____
_____
_____
_____
_____
_____
_____
_____
_____
_____
_____
_____
_____
_____
_____

**In Her Own Words**

How do you feel about your current life?
What would God say about your current life?
Why?
What can you do to make it better?

# The Notebook for the Christian Woman

When you consider the plans you have for yourself,
how do you think they align with God's plans for you?

___

## In Her Own Words

What is your definition of fun?

What is the most fun you have ever had?

Could you have fun with Jesus in the room?

Why or why not?

The Notebook for the Christian Woman

What are your favorite Christian songs?
Why?
Who do you share those with?

## In Her Own Words

What are your favorite Christian movies?

# The Notebook for the Christian Woman

What is your favorite Christian celebration?

Why?

What do you do on those days?

_____
_____
_____
_____
_____
_____
_____
_____
_____
_____
_____
_____
_____
_____
_____

# In Her Own Words

Do you write as an escape (like poetry, songs, raps or essays)?
What does this writing do to help you navigate life's journey?
How could you use your writing gifts to help God bring others to Christ?

The Notebook for the Christian Woman

Write God a love letter.

In Her Own Words

Write God a love letter, page 2.

# The Notebook for the Christian Woman

Write yourself a love letter.
Be sure to forgive yourself and affirm yourself.

## In Her Own Words

What part of your childhood will you share with your child?

Why?

Why did God allow that to happen?

What will you do to prevent those things from happening to your child?

_____
_____
_____
_____
_____
_____
_____
_____
_____
_____
_____
_____
_____
_____
_____

# The Notebook for the Christian Woman

What does God say about respect?
Define respect.
Who do you respect?
Who respects you? Do you demand respect?
Why?

_____
_____
_____
_____
_____
_____
_____
_____
_____
_____
_____
_____
_____

## In Her Own Words

What does it take to earn your respect?

How does God know that you respect Him?

List persons whom you respect.

# The Private Reconciliation of a Woman

**By Onedia N. Gage**

From caterpillar to butterfly
And you were present
And didn't know
And didn't notice

You fell for "fine" and "ok"
When she really meant "broken"
If she thought you could handle the truth
She would've answered "pained"

She transformed before your very eyes
From sweet and gentle to
Bitter and regretful
From independent and decisive to
Insecure and misunderstood
From happy and spirited to
Broken and pained

She is transforming before your very eyes
From bitter and hurt to
Powerful and overjoyed
From lonely and immobile to
Energetic and thoughtful
From disheartened and disadvantaged to
Lighthearted and refreshing

She finally reconciled the past with
Reality
She found balance
Infused strength
Reclaimed herself

In Her Own Words

Reintroduced herself to the world
As a healing vessel
Empowered herself
Transformed her thoughts
Changed her actions
Corrected her conduct

All privately
Without your attention to a single detail
All in your presence

While you stand amazed
At her private reconciliation


Reprinted from In Purple Ink: Poetry for the Spirit

# The Notebook for the Christian Woman

Define forgiveness from God's definition.

Who have you had to forgive?

Why?

_____
_____
_____
_____
_____
_____
_____
_____
_____
_____
_____
_____
_____
_____

## In Her Own Words

God forgives everything. Was it hard?

Why is it hard for you?

Jesus told us to forgive limitlessly. Why do we keep count?

Why do we hold grudges?

Could you be using the energy required to hold a grudge to honor God?

# The Notebook for the Christian Woman

Is there anyone who you have not forgiven?

Why?

Do you realize that not forgiving is a sin?

Do you consider that it takes more effort to remain unforgiving than to forgive and heal?

_____
_____
_____
_____
_____
_____
_____
_____
_____
_____
_____
_____
_____

## In Her Own Words

How long have you had a religious or spiritual life?

What faith or spiritual practices do you exercise?

Why that faith?

_____
_____
_____
_____
_____
_____
_____
_____
_____
_____
_____
_____
_____
_____
_____

Minister Gage

**The Notebook for the Christian Woman**

Define conflict.
How do you resolve conflict with others?
Is your method healthy?

## In Her Own Words

What are you addicted to?

Have you asked God to deliver you from that addiction?

Do you want to be delivered from that addiction?

_____
_____
_____
_____
_____
_____
_____
_____
_____
_____
_____
_____
_____
_____
_____

# The Notebook for the Christian Woman

What does the Bible say about the care of your body?

How would addictions contradict the body as a temple?

In Her Own Words

What are using that addiction to escape?

# The Notebook for the Christian Woman

What are the activities in which you indulge in order to escape your issues or pain (i.e. shopping, sex, drinking, etc.)? Why?
What can you do to stop those activities?

_____
_____
_____
_____
_____
_____
_____
_____
_____
_____
_____
_____
_____
_____
_____

## In Her Own Words

What is the definition of the ideal mate for you?
Who does he have to be for you to be your best you?
Did you ask God for the man He designed for you?

_____
_____
_____
_____
_____
_____
_____
_____
_____
_____
_____
_____
_____
_____

# The Notebook for the Christian Woman

What is on your "no" list (i.e. smoker, lives with mother, etc.)?

What are your relationship deal breakers (i.e. physical abuse, addicted to drugs)?

_____

_____

_____

_____

_____

_____

_____

_____

_____

_____

_____

_____

_____

_____

_____

## In Her Own Words

Are you having premarital sex or extramarital sex?

How is that affecting your relationship with Christ?

How is that sin affecting the plans God has for you?

With whom did you have sex: someone special or someone random?

Why does God not want us to have sex before marriage?

_____

_____

_____

_____

_____

_____

_____

_____

_____

_____

_____

_____

_____

_____

### The Notebook for the Christian Woman

Has being abstinent been difficult?
Do you feel comfortable and equipped to say no?
Do you know/understand that Jesus never had sex and lived for 33 years?

**In Her Own Words**

Have you ever been the mistress?
Why? What made you stop? What will make you stop?

# The Notebook for the Christian Woman

Do you send/receive nude/almost nude pictures of yourself and your mate(s)?

What would Jesus say?

What would your children/family say?

## In Her Own Words

If married, are you having regular sex with your husband?

If not, what can you do to start?

Is sex or lack thereof, impacting your relationship with your husband?

_____
_____
_____
_____
_____
_____
_____
_____
_____
_____
_____
_____
_____
_____
_____

# The Notebook for the Christian Woman

Have you ever been sexually abused, raped or molested?
Was it by someone you knew or trusted?
Who did you tell? Did the person you told believe you?
Do you know that God can heal you from that experience?
Do you want to be healed?
Do you know that God can help you forgive the person that did this to you?
Does this impact your trust for others?
Has is effected your ability to interact with your mate?

_____
_____
_____
_____
_____
_____
_____
_____
_____
_____
_____

## In Her Own Words

What does God say about homosexuality?

Do you have any gay or lesbian friends?

How do you feel about the concept?

Have you ever wondered if that is a choice versus something natural?

Has anyone ever tried to persuade you to engage in the activities that define that label?

Did God create that?

___

___

___

___

___

___

___

___

___

___

___

___

___

# The Notebook for the Christian Woman

Define self-esteem.
Do you remember that God created you in His image?
Where would yours rate on a scale of 1 to 10?
What can you do to improve your self-esteem?
Who/what can help you to improve your self-esteem?
Why does God want you to have a healthy self-esteem?

_____
_____
_____
_____
_____
_____
_____
_____
_____
_____
_____
_____

# In Her Own Words

Were you physically abused by your guardian?

How do you feel about that?

Do you understand that God can equip you to forgive them?

Do you understand that God can heal you from that hurt and pain?

_____
_____
_____
_____
_____
_____
_____
_____
_____
_____
_____
_____
_____
_____

# The Notebook for the Christian Woman

What does God want you to eat?
Could you eat healthier?
What does God say about we take into our body?

_____
_____
_____
_____
_____
_____
_____
_____
_____
_____
_____
_____
_____
_____

## In Her Own Words

Are you considered overweight?

What does God say about gluttony?

Why are you overeating?

What can you do to reduce that weight?

Is your weight affecting how you feel about yourself?

Is your weight affecting how others feel about you and treat you?

_____

_____

_____

_____

_____

_____

_____

_____

_____

_____

_____

_____

_____

_____

The Notebook for the Christian Woman

What does God say about how we spend our time?
Describe your best Saturday ever. Past or future.

### In Her Own Words

What does God have planned for you?

What will you do for the rest of your life?

# The Notebook for the Christian Woman

Do you trust God?
How do you know?
Does God trust you?
What does He trust you with?

___
___
___
___
___
___
___
___
___
___
___
___
___

## In Her Own Words

Who do you trust?

What do you trust them with?

Why?

What would have to happen to ruin your trust?

# The Notebook for the Christian Woman

How do you start your day?
How do you end the day?
How much time can you give God daily?
How will you spend time with God?
Do you have quiet or meditative time with God?

_____
_____
_____
_____
_____
_____
_____
_____
_____
_____
_____
_____
_____

### In Her Own Words

How do you spend time with God throughout the day?

How do you define a day as great or not?

# The Notebook for the Christian Woman

How does God want us to handle our anger?
What do you do to calm down after being upset?
Who do you talk to about your issue? Mentor? Peer?

_____
_____
_____
_____
_____
_____
_____
_____
_____
_____
_____
_____
_____

## In Her Own Words

Which Biblical Character would you like to meet?

Why?

_____
_____
_____
_____
_____
_____
_____
_____
_____
_____
_____
_____
_____
_____
_____
_____

# The Notebook for the Christian Woman

Which ministries are you involved in at church?

What talents do you have that you are sharing with the church?

What talents do you have that you are not sharing with the church?

_____
_____
_____
_____
_____
_____
_____
_____
_____
_____
_____
_____
_____
_____
_____

# In Her Own Words

What are your goals for your life?

Who knows these goals?

Who is helpful to hold you accountable for not quitting or keeping you from becoming discouraged?

Did God say that this was okay?

_____
_____
_____
_____
_____
_____
_____
_____
_____
_____
_____
_____
_____
_____
_____

The Notebook for the Christian Woman

What is your purpose in life?

How will you share your purpose with others?

_____
_____
_____
_____
_____
_____
_____
_____
_____
_____
_____
_____
_____
_____
_____

### In Her Own Words

How will you create a legacy worthy of your gifts?

How will you share that legacy with your children so that they have something to work toward?

What will others remember most about you?

_____
_____
_____
_____
_____
_____
_____
_____
_____
_____
_____
_____
_____
_____

How do you measure another person's investment in your life?
How do you invite others into your life?
How do you invest in the lives of others?
What does God say about investing in others?

**In Her Own Words**

Have you considered how God feels about your life?
What does God say about your personal life?
How do you feel about your life?
Why?

# The Notebook for the Christian Woman

How is your marriage?

Is marriage hard for you?

## In Her Own Words

How do you treat your husband?
Do you respect your husband?
Do you honor your husband?
Do you submit to your husband?

# The Notebook for the Christian Woman

Do you give your best to your husband all of the time?
Or does he get leftovers?
Do you plan vacations and date nights with and for your mate?

## In Her Own Words

How would you grade yourself as a wife?

How could you be a better wife?

Who helps keep you encouraged in your marriage?

Does your marriage encourage others to remain married or to get married?

_____
_____
_____
_____
_____
_____
_____
_____
_____
_____
_____
_____
_____
_____

# The Notebook for the Christian Woman

What does God say about divorce?

How many of your friends have divorced?

Are your parents divorced?

How do you feel about divorce?

Have you asked God to heal your broken heart about being divorced?

Have you asked for help if have considered divorce?

## In Her Own Words

Do you know anyone who is homeless?
Have you and your family ever been homeless?
How do you feel about homelessness?
What does God charge us to do when people are homeless, hungry or otherwise in need?
What do you propose to do about homelessness?

_____
_____
_____
_____
_____
_____
_____
_____
_____
_____
_____
_____

# The Notebook for the Christian Woman

Do you know anyone in foster care?
Do you know anyone who has been adopted?
How do you think they feel about being adopted?
How would you feel about being adopted?
What does God want us to do about those in need?
Would you help by adopting or foster parenting?

*In Her Own Words*

# THE MEASURE OF A WOMAN
## By Onedia N. Gage

The Measure of a Woman
    What is the width of her spirit
    What is the depth of her mind
    What is the weight of her heart
    What is the volume of her body
    What is the capacity of her mind
    What is the speed of her thoughts
    What is the circumference of her hugs
    What is the breadth of her love
    How many inches does she let you within the boundaries of her heart
    How many feet until she reaches forgiveness
    What is the slope of her attitude
    What is the velocity of her meekness

The Measure of a Woman
    She thinks critically
    She plans carefully
    She speaks dynamically
    She loves passionately
    She lives authentically
    She moves fearlessly
    She leads humbly
    She fears God

Experience the Measure of a Woman
    Her love
    Her fears
    Her tears
    Her victories
    Her power
    Her influence

### The Notebook for the Christian Woman

Her motivation

Invest in the Measure of a Woman
- Create for her a loving environment
- Create for her a safe place

Go the distance for the Measure of a Woman

The Measure of a Woman
- Defines love
- Defies opposition
- Declares independence
- Decorates hearts
- Demands chemistry

### The Measure of a Woman

Reprinted from <u>The Measure of a Woman: The Details of Her Soul</u>

## Reflections

The Notebook for the Christian Woman

## Reflections

## Reflections

The Notebook for the Christian Woman

## Reflections

# Appendix

| | |
|---|---|
| Your Testimony | 183 |
| The Names of God | 185 |
| Prayer Directions | 187 |
| Prayer Request List/Journal | 188 |
| Favorite Scriptures | 193 |
| Goals | 200 |
| Mission | 202 |
| Vision | 205 |
| Values | 209 |
| Dreams | 211 |

The Notebook for the Christian Woman

In Her Own Words

# Your Testimony

Your testimony is your experience with God and the results of that experience. This includes your first encounter with Christ to your current life.

Consider the answers to the following questions to develop your testimony:
1. When did you first meet Christ?
2. How do you share how you met Christ with others?
3. What have your encounters with God been like?
4. What is your relationship with God like?
5. What danger has He kept you from?
6. What have you done that would have sabotaged God's work if He had not stopped you?
7. What has happened that you realized that only God was in charge to make this happen?

_____
_____
_____
_____
_____
_____
_____
_____
_____
_____
_____
_____

The Notebook for the Christian Woman

# The Names of God

(1) **Elohim**: The plural form of *EL*, meaning "strong one." It is used of false gods, but when used of the true God, it is a plural of majesty and intimates the trinity. It is especially used of God's sovereignty, creative work, mighty work for Israel and in relation to His sovereignty (Isa. 54:5; Jer. 32:27; Gen. 1:1; Isa. 45:18; Deut. 5:23; 8:15; Ps. 68:7).

Compounds of *El*:

- *El Shaddai:* "God Almighty." The derivation is uncertain. Some think it stresses God's loving supply and comfort; others His power as the Almighty one standing on a mountain and who corrects and chastens (Gen. 17:1; 28:3; 35:11; Ex. 6:1; Ps. 91:1, 2).
- *El Elyon:* "The Most High God." Stresses God's strength, sovereignty, and supremacy (Gen. 14:19; Ps. 9:2; Dan. 7:18, 22, 25).
- *El Olam*: "The Everlasting God." Emphasizes God's unchangeableness and is connected with His inexhaustibleness (Gen. 16:13).

(2) **Yahweh (YHWH):** Comes from a verb which means "to exist, be." This, plus its usage, shows that this name stresses God as the independent and self-existent God of revelation and redemption (Gen. 4:3; Ex. 6:3 (cf. 3:14); 3:12).

Compounds of *Yahweh*: Strictly speaking, these compounds are designations or titles which reveal additional facts about God's character.

- *Yahweh Jireh (Yireh):* "The Lord will provide." Stresses God's provision for His people (Gen. 22:14).
- *Yahweh Nissi:* "The Lord is my Banner." Stresses that God is our rallying point and our means of victory; the one who fights for His people (Ex. 17:15).
- *Yahweh Shalom:* "The Lord is Peace." Points to the Lord as the means of our peace and rest (Jud. 6:24).
- *Yahweh Sabbaoth:* "The Lord of Hosts." A military figure portraying the Lord as the commander of the armies of heaven (1 Sam. 1:3; 17:45).
- *Yahweh Maccaddeshcem:* "The Lord your Sanctifier." Portrays the Lord as our means of sanctification or as the one who sets believers apart for His purposes (Ex. 31:13).
- *Yahweh Ro'i:* "The Lord my Shepherd." Portrays the Lord as the Shepherd who cares for His people as a shepherd cares for the sheep of his pasture (Ps. 23:1).
- *Yahweh Tsidkenu*: "The Lord our Righteousness." Portrays the Lord as the means of our righteousness (Jer. 23:6).

- ***Yahweh Shammah***: "The Lord is there." Portrays the Lord's personal presence in the millennial kingdom (Ezek. 48:35).
- ***Yahweh Elohim Israel:*** "The Lord, the God of Israel." Identifies Yahweh as the God of Israel in contrast to the false gods of the nations (Jud. 5:3.; Isa. 17:6).

(3) ***Adonai:*** Like *Elohim*, this too is a plural of majesty. The singular form means "master, owner." Stresses man's relationship to God as his master, authority, and provider (Gen. 18:2; 40:1; 1 Sam. 1:15; Ex. 21:1-6; Josh. 5:14).

(4) ***Theos***: Greek word translated "God." Primary name for God used in the New Testament. Its use teaches: (1) *He is the only true God* (Matt. 23:9; Rom. 3:30); (2) *He is unique* (1 Tim. 1:17; John 17:3; Rev. 15:4; 16:7); (3) *He is transcendent* (Acts 17:24; Heb. 3:4; Rev. 10:6); (4) *He is the Savior* (John 3:16; 1 Tim. 1:1; 2:3; 4:10). This name is used of Christ as God in John 1:1, 18; 20:28; 1 John 5:20; Tit. 2:13; Rom. 9:5; Heb. 1:8; 2 Pet. 1:1.

(5) ***Kurios***: Greek word translated "Lord." Stresses authority and supremacy. While it can mean sir (John 4:11), owner (Luke 19:33), master (Col. 3:22), or even refer to idols (1 Cor. 8:5) or husbands (1 Pet. 3:6), it is used mostly as the equivalent of *Yahweh* of the Old Testament. It too is used of Jesus Christ meaning (1) Rabbi or Sir (Matt. 8:6); (2) God or Deity (John 20:28; Acts 2:36; Rom. 10:9; Phil. 2:11).

(6) ***Despotes***: Greek word translated "Master." Carries the idea of ownership while *kurios* stressed supreme authority (Luke 2:29; Acts 4:24; Rev. 6:10; 2 Pet. 2:1; Jude 4).

(7) ***Father***: A distinctive New Testament revelation is that through faith in Christ, God becomes our personal Father. Father is used of God in the Old Testament only 15 times while it is used of God 245 times in the New Testament. As a name of God, it stresses God's loving care, provision, discipline, and the way we are to address God in prayer (Matt. 7:11; Jam. 1:17; Heb. 12:5-11; John 15:16; 16:23; Eph. 2:18; 3:15; 1 Thess. 3:11).

Source: http://www.agapebiblestudy.com/documents/the%20many%20names%20of%20god.htm

# Prayer
# A Short How To Guide

The prayers which are most effective follow the following "rules:"

- It is a conversation with God.
- Be Honest with God.
- This is a relationship.
- God is to be praised, worshiped and glorified.
- God likes His word prayed back to Him.
- This is not a list of stuff you want.
- Think of more than yourself when you pray.
- Be authentic with God and yourself.
- Be prepared for people to ask you about your prayer life and faith.
- Do not worry about big words or long sentences.
- Please know that God is not taking revenge on others for you, and vice versa.
- Please prayer in the name of Jesus.
- There is no correct way to pray.

## Scriptures on Prayer

Matthew 6:9-14

1 Thessalonians 5:17

Matthew 26:

John 17

The Notebook for the Christian Woman

## Prayer Requests
## Prayer Journal

1. What are you asking God for?
2. What are you hoping God will do?
3. What are you expecting from God?
4. What has God already done to exceed your expectations?
5. What has God done to get your attention?
6. What has He shown about Himself and you?

_____
_____
_____
_____
_____
_____
_____
_____
_____
_____

## In Her Own Words

The Notebook for the Christian Woman

In Her Own Words

The Notebook for the Christian Woman

## Favorite Scriptures

**Numbers 6:24-26**

[24] The LORD bless you and keep you;
[25] the LORD make his face shine on you and be gracious to you;
[26] the LORD turn his face toward you and give you peace."

**Jeremiah 1:5**

[5] "Before I formed you in the womb I knew[a] you, before you were born I set you apart; I appointed you as a prophet to the nations."

**Jeremiah 29:11**

[11] For I know the plans I have for you," declares the LORD, "plans to prosper you and not to harm you, plans to give you hope and a future.

**Psalm 8:1**

[1] LORD, our Lord, how excellent is Your name in all the earth!

**Psalm 19:14**

[14] May these words of my mouth and this meditation of my heart be pleasing in your sight, LORD, my Rock and my Redeemer.

# The Notebook for the Christian Woman

**Psalm 46:1, 10**

[1] God is our refuge and strength, an ever-present help in trouble. [10] "Be still, and know that I am God."

**Psalm 119:11**

[11] I have hidden your word in my heart that I might not sin against you.

**Psalm 139:14**

[14] I praise you because I am fearfully and wonderfully made; your works are wonderful, I know that full well.

**Proverbs 3:5-6**

[5] Trust in the LORD with all your heart and lean not on your own understanding;
[6] in all your ways acknowledge him, and he will make your paths straight.

**Proverbs 23:7 (KJV)**

[7] For as he thinketh in his heart, so is he: Eat and drink, saith he to thee; but his heart is not with thee.

**Habakkuk 2:2**

[2] Then the LORD replied: "Write down the revelation and make it plain on tablets so that a herald[a] may run with it.

**Matthew 11:28, 30**

[28] "Come to me, all you who are weary and heavy-ladened, and I will give you rest.

[30] For my yoke is easy and my burden is light."

**Matthew 14:31**

[31] Immediately Jesus reached out his hand and caught him. "You of little faith," he said, "why did you doubt?"

**Matthew 22:37**

[37] Jesus replied: "'Love the Lord your God with all your heart and with all your soul and with all your mind.

**Matthew 28:19-20**

[19] Therefore go and make disciples of all nations, baptizing them in[a] the name of the Father and of the Son and of the Holy Spirit, [20] and teaching them to obey everything I have commanded you. And surely I am with you always, to the very end of the age."

**Luke 9:24**

[23] Then he said to them all: "If anyone would come after me, he must deny himself and take up his cross daily and follow me. [24] For whoever wants to save his life will lose it, but whoever loses his life for me will save it.

**Luke 23:34**

[34] Jesus said, "Father, forgive them, for they do not know what they are doing."[a] And they divided up his clothes by casting lots.

**John 1:1-2**

[1] In the beginning was the Word, and the Word was with God, and the Word was God. [2] He was with God in the beginning.

# The Notebook for the Christian Woman

**John 3:16**

[16] "For God so loved the world that he gave his one and only Son,[a] that whoever believes in him shall not perish but have eternal life.

**John 3:30**

[30] He must become greater; I must become less.

**John 11:35**

[35] Jesus wept.

**Romans 8:26**

[26] In the same way, the Spirit helps us in our weakness. We do not know what we ought to pray for, but the Spirit himself intercedes for us with groans that words cannot express.

**1 Corinthians 10:13**

[13] No temptation has seized you except what is common to man. And God is faithful; he will not let you be tempted beyond what you can bear. But when you are tempted, he will also provide a way out so that you can stand up under it.

**Galatians 5:22-23**

[22] But the fruit of the Spirit is love, joy, peace, patience, kindness, goodness, faithfulness, [23] gentleness and self-control. Against such things there is no law.

**Ephesians 3:14-21**

[14] For this reason I kneel before the Father, [15] from whom his whole family[a] in heaven and on earth derives its name. [16] I pray that out of his glorious riches he may strengthen you with power through his Spirit in your inner being, [17] so that Christ may dwell in your hearts through faith. And I pray that you, being rooted and established in love, [18] may have power, together with all the saints, to grasp how wide and long and high and deep is the love of Christ, [19] and to know this love that surpasses knowledge—that you may be filled to the measure of all the fullness of God. [20] Now unto him who is able to do immeasurably more than all we ask or imagine, according to his power that is at work within us, [21] to him be glory in the church and in Christ Jesus throughout all generations, for ever and ever! Amen.

**Ephesians 4:26-27**

[26] "In your anger do not sin"[a]: Do not let the sun go down while you are still angry, [27] and do not give the devil a foothold.

**Ephesians 4:32**

[32] Be kind and compassionate to one another, forgiving each other, just as in Christ God forgave you.

**Philippians 4:7**

[7] And the peace of God, which transcends all understanding, will guard your hearts and your minds in Christ Jesus.

**Philippians 4:13-17**

[13] I can do everything through him who gives me strength. [14] Yet it was good of you to share in my troubles. [15] Moreover, as you Philippians know, in the early days of your acquaintance with the gospel, when I set out from Macedonia, not one church shared with me in the matter of giving and receiving, except you only; [16] for even when I

was in Thessalonica, you sent me aid again and again when I was in need. [17] Not that I am looking for a gift, but I am looking for what may be credited to your account.

**Colossians 3:23**

[23] Whatever you do, work at it with all your heart, as working for the Lord, not for men,

**1 Thessalonians 5:17**

[17] pray continually;

**Hebrews 11:6**

[6] And without faith it is impossible to please God, because anyone who comes to him must believe that he exists and that he rewards those who earnestly seek him.

**Hebrews 13:5b**

[5] Keep your lives free from the love of money and be content with what you have, because God has said, "Never will I leave you; never will I forsake you."

**James 1:2-5**

[2] Consider it pure joy, my brothers, whenever you face trials of many kinds, [3] because you know that the testing of your faith develops perseverance. [4] Perseverance must finish its work so that you may be mature and complete, not lacking anything. [5] If any of you lacks wisdom, he should ask God, who gives generously to all without finding fault, and it will be given to him.

**Jude 24**

[24] Now unto him that is able to keep you from falling, and to present you faultless before the presence of his glory with exceeding joy,

**Revelation 3:16**

[16] So, because you are lukewarm—neither hot nor cold—I am about to spit you out of my mouth.

The Notebook for the Christian Woman

# Goals

**goal** [gohl] *noun*

the result or achievement toward <u>which</u> effort is directed; aim; end.

The questions that you answer when developing goals are as follows:

1. What do I want to accomplish for God, with God, because of God?
2. When do I want to accomplish this by? What does God's timing look like?
3. Who is going to help me and hold me accountable? Who has God sent my way for this matter?
4. What do you do when you do not meet the goals as planned? What will God do in the meantime?
5. Who do you share your successes with? How will God use my achievement to help others?

In Her Own Words

## Goals

| Goals | By When | Who |
|---|---|---|
| | | |

The Notebook for the Christian Woman

# Mission Statement

A personal mission statement is based on habit 2 of <u>7 Habits of Highly Effective People</u> called begin with the end in mind. In ones life, the most effective way to begin with the end in mind is to develop a mission statement one that focuses what you want to be in terms of character and what you want to do in reference to contribution of achievements. Writing a mission statement can be the most important activity an individual can take to truly lead ones life.

Victor Hugo once said there is nothing as powerful as an idea whose time has finally come, you may call it a credo, a philosophy, you may call it a purpose statement, it's not as important as to what you call it, no it's how you define your definition. That mission and vision statement is more powerful, more significant, more influential, than the baggage of the past, or even the accumulated noise of the present.

What is a mission statement you ask? Personal mission statements based on correct principles are like a personal constitution, the basis for making major, life-directing decisions, the basis for making daily decisions in the midst of the circumstances and emotions that affect our lives.

Your statement may be a few words or several pages, but it is not a "to do" list. It reflects your uniqueness and must speak to you powerfully about the person you are and the person you are becoming.

**Why should you write a personal mission statement?**

Numerous experts on leadership and personal development emphasize how vital it is for you to craft your own personal vision for your life. Warren Bennis, Stephen Covey, Peter Senge, and others point out that a powerful vision can help you succeed far beyond where you'd be without one. That vision can propel you and inspire those around you to reach their own dreams.

Q: How do I go about creating my Personal Mission Statement?

A: A Mission Statement is defined as having goals and a deadline. This is opposed to the notion that a Mission Statement is just a bunch of flowery, general phrases like, "I will be the best business person I can be."

**What should you include when writing a great personal mission statement?**

- describe your best characteristics and how you express them
- have specific, measurable outcomes (or goals)
- have a deadline — for example, December 31st 2012, or a year from today.

When Stephen Covey talks about 'mission statement' in this quote, he is referring to the articulation of your life purpose. "If you don't set your goals based upon your Mission Statement, you may be climbing the ladder of success only to realize, when you get to the top, you're on the WRONG BUILDING." **Stephen Covey – 7 Habits of Highly Effective People.**

**Mission Statement Example – Poor (It's more like a Vision Statement)**

"I aspire to start my own business. I want to help others and be a better businesswoman. I will deliver the best food with the highest service levels." Jane

**Mission Statement Example – Better**

"I will start my business within 3 months and plan to grow it to $500,000 in revenues within a year. Using this success, my staff and I will spread the word to local schools and businesses about eco-friendly food production in order that we reach at least 100 people within the same time frame. My purpose will be to massively add value to our local community in measurable ways that have a real impact on people's health now and in the future," Jane.

**What to do with your Mission Statement?**

So now we have a mission, we can set a range of goals on the road to achieving your outcomes and dreams. Your values are clarified and should be in line with the goals you want to achieve in life so you should find it easier to make decisions and to do the "right thing" because you can simply ask yourself, "Will this help me achieve my mission?"

You can even put your mission statement in an area where your family or even co-workers will see it. For, a mission statement defines who you are and what you stand for. This lets people see how you think and feel, which in turn, will help them respect, think and act in line with your values too.

The Notebook for the Christian Woman

## Mission Statement

_____
_____
_____
_____
_____
_____
_____
_____
_____
_____
_____
_____
_____
_____
_____
_____

## Vision Statement

A personal vision/mission statement is the framework for creating a powerful life.

*Your personal vision statement provides the direction necessary to guide the course of your days and the choices you make about your life.*

The idea is to craft a broad based idea about your life and what will really make it exciting and fulfilling, that's your life vision.

From the vision, you craft a more focused and action orientated "mission" statement based on "purpose." And finally you get to a list of goals, wishes, desires and needs.

In his book 'The Success Principles,' Jack Canfield tells us that in order to create a balanced and successful life; your vision needs to include the following seven areas:

1. work and career
2. finances
3. recreation and free time
4. health and fitness
5. relationships
6. personal goals
7. contribution to the larger community

It does not include the distinctive ways that you intend to accomplish your purpose.

**Why Write a Personal Vision Statement?**

To express:

- your purpose
- your life's dream
- your core values & beliefs
- what you want for yourself

- what you want to contribute to others
- what you want to be

**Characteristics of a Vision Statement:**

- Engages your heart & spirit
- Taps into embedded concerns & needs
- Asserts what you want to create
- Is something worth going for
- Provides meaning to the work you do
- Is a little cloudy and grand
- Is simple
- Is a living document
- Provides a starting place from which to get more specificity
- Is based on quality and dedication

**Key Elements of a Vision Statement:**

- Written down and referred to daily
- Written in present tense, as if it has already been completed
- Includes a variety of activities and time frames
- Filled with descriptive details that anchor it to reality

**What Visions Are Not:**

- A mission statement: "Why do we exist now?"
- A strategic plan: "How do we plan to get there?"
- A set of objectives: "We will accomplish X by Y time to Z% target audience."

**Use these questions to guide your thoughts:**

- What are the ten things you most enjoy doing? Be honest. These are the ten things without which your weeks, months, and years would feel incomplete.
- What three things must you do every single day to feel fulfilled in your work?
- What are your five-six most important values?

- Your life has a number of important facets or dimensions, all of which deserve some attention in your personal vision statement.
- Write one important goal for each of them: physical, spiritual, work or career, family, social relationships, financial security, mental improvement and attention, and fun.
- If you never had to work another day in your life, how would you spend your time instead of working?
- When your life is ending, what will you regret not doing, seeing, or achieving?
- What strengths have other people commented on about you and your accomplishments? What strengths do you see in yourself?

The Notebook for the Christian Woman

## Vision Statement

In Her Own Words

## Values Statement

A personal **value** is <u>absolute or relative and ethical value</u>, the assumption of which can be the basis for ethical action. A *value system* is a set of consistent <u>values</u> and measures. A *principle value* is a foundation upon which other values and measures of <u>integrity</u> are based.

Some values are physiologically determined and are normally considered objective, such as a desire to avoid physical pain or to seek pleasure. Other values are considered <u>subjective</u>, vary across individuals and cultures, and are in many ways aligned with <u>belief</u> and belief systems. Types of values include <u>ethical</u>/<u>moral</u> values, <u>doctrinal</u>/<u>ideological</u> (religious, political) values, <u>social</u> values, and <u>aesthetic</u> values. It is debated whether some values that are not clearly physiologically determined, such as <u>altruism</u>, are <u>intrinsic</u>, and whether some, such as acquisitiveness, should be classified as <u>vices</u> or <u>virtues</u>. Values have been studied in various disciplines: <u>anthropology</u>, <u>behavioral economics</u>, <u>business ethics</u>, <u>corporate governance</u>, <u>moral philosophy</u>, <u>political sciences</u>, <u>social psychology</u>, <u>sociology</u> and <u>theology</u> to name a few.

Values can be defined as broad preference concerning appropriate courses of action or outcomes. As such, values reflect a person's sense of right and wrong or what "ought" to be. "Equal rights for all", "Excellence deserves admiration", and "People should be treated with respect and dignity" are representative of values. Values tend to influence attitudes and behavior.

The Notebook for the Christian Woman

## Values Statement

In Her Own Words

## Dreams List

The Notebook for the Christian Woman

## In Her Own Words

The Notebook for the Christian Woman

## Resources

www.onediagage.com
As We Grow Together Daily Devotional for Expectant Couples
As We Grow Together Prayer Journal for Expectant Couples
The Blue Print: Poetry for the Soul
From Two to One: The Notebook for Couples
In Purple Ink: Poetry for the Spirit
Living a Whole Life: Sermons which Prompt, Provoke and Promote Life
Love Letters to God from a Teenage Girl
The Measure of a Woman: The Details of Her Soul
The Notebook: For Me, About Me, By Me
The Notebook for the Christian Teen
On This Journey Daily Devotional for Young People
On This Journey Prayer Journal for Young People
One Day More Than We Deserve Daily Devotional for the Growing Christian
One Day More Than We Deserve Prayer Journal for the Growing Christian
Promises, Promises: A Christian Novel
Tools for These Times: Timely Sermons for Uncertain Times
With An Anointed Voice: The Power of Prayer
Yielded and Submitted: A Woman's Journey for a Life Dedicated to God
Yielded and Submitted: A Woman's Journey for a Life Dedicated to God Prayers and Journal
Yielded and Submitted: A Woman's Journey for a Life Dedicated to God An Intimate Study
The Power of a Praying Woman Stormie Omartian
The Power of a Praying Wife Stormie Omartian
Discerning the Voice of God Priscilla Shrirer
Kingdom Woman Tony Evans and Crystal Evans Hurst

The Notebook for the Christian Woman

# Acknowledgements

God, thank You for Your plans for me. Thank You for ***In Her Own Words: The Notebook For the Christian Woman,*** and choosing me to complete Your project. I just want to please You, God. Thank You for continuing to anoint me and to invest in me and my gifts, which keep surprising me. Thank You for loving and forgiving me.

Hillary and Nehemiah, thank you for supporting me and my endeavors. Thank you for loving me, especially when I do nothing without a pen and a clipboard, thank you for enduring my late nights, your ideas, the sounding board, the love and the support. Thank you for celebrating our legacy.

To my editor, Kim Joiner. Thank you for reading and answering the questions and editing those errors and clarifying those unclear areas. Your time, effort and contribution mean a lot to me.

To my prayer partners and to my accountability partners, thank you for the long talks and the powerful prayers and the encouragement.

To the readers who this will reach and empower and touch and affect, may these words empower you and help you reach some resolve. May you be inspired to achieve your goals and dreams. May you enhance your relationship with God so that your other relationships will also improve. May you enhance your self-esteem through prayer and study. May you have courage and peace. Share love the best you can until you can share love without reservation.

The Notebook for the Christian Woman

In Her Own Words

## About the Inquisitive One

The author believes that questions help you to grow and create the appropriate amount of challenge.
Do not hesitate to ask, to engage at a high level of participation, anticipating God's best for you!
@onediangage (twitter) ♦ onediagage@onediagage.com ♦ facebook.com/onediagageministries
youtube.com/onediagage ♦ blogtalkradio.com/onediagage ♦ ongage (instagram)
www.onediagage.com

The Notebook for the Christian Woman

## PREACHER ♦ TEACHER ♦ FACILITATOR
## CONFERENCE SPEAKER ♦ PANELIST ♦ WORKSHOP LEADER

To invite Ms. Gage to speak at your church, youth group, or youth ministry,
Please contact us at: www.onedigage.com
@onediangage (twitter) ♦ onediagage@onediagage.com ♦ facebook.com/onediagageministries
youtube.com/onediagage ♦ blogtalkradio.com/onediagage

The Notebook for the Christian Woman

In Her Own Words

## Publishing

Do you have a book you want to write, but do not know what to do?
Do you have a book you need to publish but do not know how to start?
Would publishing move your career forward?

Let us help

onediagage@purpleink.net ♦ www.purpleink.net

**713.705.5530 ♦ 512.715.4243**

www.ingramcontent.com/pod-product-compliance
Lightning Source LLC
Chambersburg PA
CBHW080448170426
43196CB00016B/2729